The Bar and Bat Mitzvah Manual

Six Steps to a Memorable Family Celebration

Rabbi Steven M. Bob and Lisa Bob Howard

Editorial Committee

Sara L. Blumstein

Rabbi Martin S. Cohen

Lauren Resnikoff

BEHRMAN HOUSE, INC.
www.behrmanhouse.com

Letter from the Authors

Mazal tov! Your family is about to celebrate one of Judaism's most momentous life-cycle events—bar and bat mitzvah. After much preparation and anticipation, the ceremony you have long imagined is almost within reach.

This handbook will build your comfort with the key elements of bar and bat mitzvah. It will help your family work together to create a meaningful celebration. And it will highlight the long-term investment this rite of passage into Jewish adulthood can become for you as individuals and as a Jewish family.

Together you will explore the history and significance of the ceremony itself, the tradition of reading the Torah and the Prophets, the key elements of the prayer service, different mitzvah projects, how to create a celebration that reflects your family values and commitments, and how to make the best parts of the day—and the values they embody—last forever.

We hope that your celebration is full of joy. May it lead to everlasting rewards for your family, your guests, and the entire community.

Rabbi Steven M. Bob & Lisa Bob Howard

What is a Bar and Bat Mitzvah?

By the end of this workshop, your family will be able to:

▶ Place your family's celebration in a historical context—when and where were the first bar and bat mitzvah?

▶ Explain the terms bar mitzvah, bat mitzvah, b'nai mitzvah, and b'not mitzvah

▶ Explore what makes the bar or bat mitzvah ceremony significant for your family

Lesson Launch

The following story is a midrash—an elaboration on a Torah text. Read the midrash aloud with the other members of your b'nai mitzvah class.

Jewish tradition teaches that when our forefather Abraham was a child, he worked in an idol shop that belonged to his father, Terach. One day when Abraham was left to mind the shop, he destroyed all of the idols except for the biggest one. Terach returned and asked Abraham what had happened. His son explained that the largest idol had become angry and smashed the others.

"The idols are made of clay! They cannot smash each other," objected Terach.

Abraham replied, "If you know that they are only clay objects, why do you worship them?"

The rabbis tell us that Abraham was thirteen years old when he smashed the idols.

From the time of Abraham until today, adolescence has always been a time for questioning. Young adults begin to question rules and develop their own beliefs.

As a family, discuss what aspects—both physical and emotional—of being thirteen allowed Abraham to act as he did. List three answers in the space below.

1. _____

2. _____

3. _____

Jewish tradition teaches that parents are responsible for their children's fulfillment of Jewish laws until the day of their thirteenth birthday on the Jewish calendar. At thirteen—twelve for girls—the rabbis teach, young Jewish men and women become responsible for their own fulfillment of Jewish laws. They are ready to consider the ethical and moral significance of each mitzvah (literally, "commandment"—plural, *mitzvot*). And, they are ready to participate fully in all areas of Jewish life, such as being called up to the Torah for an *aliyah* or being counted as part of a prayer minyan, the quorum of ten Jewish adults required for some religious services.

Hebrew Helper

The Hebrew term "bar mitzvah" (plural, b'nai mitzvah) is literally translated as "son of the commandment." Similarly, "bat mitzvah" (plural, b'not mitzvah) means "daughter of the commandment." The plural "b'nai mitzvah" is used when collectively referring to boys and girls.

The terms bar mitzvah and bat mitzvah are used in two ways:

1. To describe the young person who is undergoing the transition to Jewish religious adulthood

2. To describe the ceremony that marks this transition

How the Bar Mitzvah Began

As early as 800 CE, some Jewish boys marked their thirteenth birthdays by reading from the Torah. This practice publicly acknowledged the boys' new status as active members of the Jewish community. By the 1500s, it had become common practice for boys to read from the Torah on the Shabbat immediately following their thirteenth birthdays. By the 1600s, a ritual meal had become part of the celebration.

Today's bar mitzvah ceremony incorporates both Torah reading and a celebratory meal.

The First Bat Mitzvah

In the 1800s, some Eastern Europeans began to mark the occasion of a young woman's becoming bat mitzvah with a private celebratory meal.

The first public bat mitzvah ceremony in the United States was celebrated by Rabbi Mordecai Kaplan's daughter, Judith, in 1922. Rabbi Kaplan was the founder and leader of today's Reconstructionist Jewish movement. Like boys her age, Judith read from the Torah and recited the Torah blessings—practices not previously performed publicly by women.

Today, egalitarian congregations celebrate both the bar mitzvah and bat mitzvah with similar rituals.

D'var Torah

During the bar and bat mitzvah ceremony, many teens offer a short speech called a *d'var Torah* (literally a "word of Torah," a lesson interpreting a holy text), or *d'rashah* (an explanation or sermon). In their *divrei Torah*, (plural of *d'var Torah*), b'nai mitzvah discuss the parts of the Torah portion or haftarah that they find personally significant. Many teens also talk about what their bar or bat mitzvah means to them—new responsibilities (some easy, some hard), such as reading from the Torah for the first time; new chances to fulfill a mitzvah, such as tutoring other students or fasting on Yom Kippur; and new ways that they and others see their roles in the community, for example, becoming a *madrich* or *madrichah* (teacher's aide). You will learn more about the *d'var Torah* in Workshop 2.

What Does Bar and Bat Mitzvah Mean Today?

A midrash teaches that when God offered the Torah to the Jewish people at Mount Sinai, they accepted by replying, *"Na'aseh, v'nishma"*—"We will do, and we will listen."

During the bar or bat mitzvah ceremony, it is as if each teen is standing at Mount Sinai and personally asserting, "Yes, I will accept the Torah." The ceremony announces that these young Jewish men and women are not only Jewish in name but also in deed.

In addition to the bar or bat mitzvah ceremony, what are some of the other ways b'nai mitzvah and b'not mitzvah can demonstrate their commitment to their families, their community, the Jewish people, and God? List some of your answers in the spaces provided below.

1. Family

_____

_____

_____

2. Jewish community

_____

_____

_____

3. Jewish people

_____

_____

_____

4. God

_____

_____

_____

TeenTalk

Your bar or bat mitzvah marks a time when your family *and* your community offer you greater responsibility.

Your family trusts you to be more independent and to make smart choices, such as handing in your schoolwork on time or choosing your friends wisely.

As a teenager, you will spend more time without adult supervision. You will have to make choices on your own—without your parents' help and while being influenced by your friends.

Describe a situation at home, in school, or with your friends in which you might be required to make a sensible choice about how to act. What would you do in that situation?

_____

_____

_____

When you become a bar or bat mitzvah, your Jewish community entrusts you with the responsibilities of leading the congregation in prayer and explaining the meaning of the Torah portion.

In what other ways does the community express its confidence in you during your bar or bat mitzvah ceremony?

_____

_____

_____

_____

Bar and Bat Mitzvah Checklist

Put a check mark next to two responsibilities that you already have. Choose two responsibilities that you would like to take on. Draw a star next to these two actions.

☐ Tidying your room and making your bed

☐ Keeping track of school assignments

☐ Writing thank-you notes

☐ Helping care for a younger sibling or other child

☐ Attending synagogue services

☐ Making a commitment to a school club, sports team, or synagogue youth group

☐ Taking care of a pet

☐ Attending Hebrew high school or confirmation classes

☐ Getting to or from school (including walking, riding a bike, or taking a bus)

☐ Getting to or from friends' houses

☐ Participating in Jewish holiday observances, such as fasting on Yom Kippur

☐ Keeping track of allowance or other spending money, or creating a personal budget

☐ Doing *g'milut ḥasadim*—acts of loving-kindness—such as visiting a senior center or animal shelter, helping out a local charity, or cleaning up the local park

G'milut Ḥasadim

A young person who has reached the age of bar or bat mitzvah can lead services, read from the Torah, and be counted in a minyan. In addition to these mitzvot of worship *(avodah)*, b'nai mitzvah have a new responsibility for mitzvot of *g'milut ḥasadim* (acts of loving-kindness), such as visiting the sick, welcoming guests, and feeding the hungry. B'nai mitzvah are old enough to make a positive difference in the communities in which they live.

The story below tells how one boy made a difference for the homeless population in Philadelphia.

The Real World

At eleven years old, Trevor Ferrell was shaken by a television news piece about homeless people in his home city of Philadelphia. He convinced his parents to take him downtown to bring blankets to people sleeping out in the cold.

Night after night, Trevor and his parents took blankets to homeless people. Trevor also visited his local newspaper to ask if it would print a notice asking for donations of blankets and clothes. The newspaper ran a feature story, and the story was picked up by national media, including *The New York Times*. Within one month of Trevor's first trip downtown, his story had made national news, prompting donations from all over the country. The generosity of many people led to the opening of Trevor's Place, a seventeen-bedroom residence that to this day provides shelter, food, clothing, and employment training for homeless men, women, and children in Philadelphia.

Trevor's story demonstrates that young people can effect change in their communities. His efforts were successful largely because of his initiative and determination and because of the support of his parents.

Many students begin mitzvah projects as they prepare to become b'nai mitzvah. These projects often focus on social issues such as homelessness, public health, and animal rights. As a family, discuss the social issues—large and small—about which each of you is concerned, then list them below.

_____

_____

_____

_____

_____

_____

Parent's Perspective

Becoming a bar or bat mitzvah marks a new phase in your child's life. It also signals a new stage in your own life. Your place in the constellation of your larger family has shifted.

If this is your first child to reach the age of bar or bat mitzvah, then this may be the first life-cycle event for your extended family for which you are responsible. Just as your child faces new opportunities and new responsibilities, so do you; for example, in making the detailed plans often required for this event.

Below, identify one new opportunity for you, the parent, as your child becomes a bar or bat mitzvah, and one new responsibility.

New opportunity:

_____

_____

New responsibility:

_____

_____

Focus on Text

וְאָמַרְתָּ אֲלֵהֶם וְעָשׂוּ לָהֶם צִיצִת עַל־כַּנְפֵי בִגְדֵיהֶם...
וּרְאִיתֶם אֹתוֹ וּזְכַרְתֶּם אֶת־כָּל־מִצְוֹת יְיָ וַעֲשִׂיתֶם אֹתָם...

*Instruct them to make for themselves fringes
on the corners of their garments... look at it and recall
the commandments of the Eternal and do them...*

—Numbers 15:38–39

The Torah teaches us to put fringes on the corners of our garments so that we will look at them and recall the commandments. Today, these fringes, or *tzitziyot* (plural of *tzitzit*), are put onto the four corners of a tallit. On the occasion of the bar or bat mitzvah, the teen may use a tallit for the first time.

A *tzitzit* (צִיצִית) has eight strings and five knots—in total, thirteen, the age of bar or bat mitzvah. Jewish tradition assigns every Hebrew letter a numerical value. To find the numerical value of the word *tzitzit*, add together the value of each letter in the word: *tzadee* (צ) 90 + *yud* (י) 10 + *tzadee* (צ) 90 + *yud* (י) 10 + *tav* (ת) 400= 600. Add to that 13, the number of knots and strings, and the grand total is 613, the number of mitzvot, tradition teaches, that are in the Torah. In this way, the fringes of our *tallitot* (plural of "tallit") remind us of the 613 mitzvot.

Teen Talk

Wearing a tallit reminds us not to forget the many mitzvot in the Torah. Do you plan to wear a tallit at your bar or bat mitzvah? If so, what tallit will you wear to fulfill this special commandment? Perhaps you will buy a new tallit that you will continue to wear for many years to come. Maybe you will wear a tallit that was once worn by another family member at his or her bar or bat mitzvah. You might also wear a tallit belonging to your congregation, signifying your ties to your community. Deciding if you are going to wear a tallit and which tallit to wear are important decisions, ones that you might wish to discuss as a family.

Reflections

In this workshop, you have learned about the historical and contemporary significance of the bar and bat mitzvah. But what of its personal significance?

The occasion of a bar or bat mitzvah is important to your family, but the significance may vary a great deal depending on your family's background. For example, if everyone in your family—mother, father, grandmother, and grandfather—celebrated becoming b'nai mitzvah in America, the bar or bat mitzvah may be symbolic of Jewish continuity. In other families, the bar or bat mitzvah is symbolic of a bold step forward. For example, if your family has a member who converted to Judaism, the bar or bat mitzvah might signify a new beginning for your family.

As a family, discuss how your experience compares to that of previous generations in your family. Use the space below to jot down your reflections.

The Torah Connection

By the end of this workshop, your family will be able to:

▶ Navigate the five books of the Torah

▶ Explain the difference between a Torah portion and a haftarah

▶ Identify the Torah portion that the bar or bat mitzvah will read along with its main lessons, themes, and personal relevance

Lesson Launch

*It is a tree of life to those who hold fast to it,
and all its supporters are happy.*

—Proverbs 3:18

In the Book of Proverbs, the Torah is called a "tree of life," an *etz ḥayyim*. As a family, brainstorm answers to the following question. Record your ideas on the lines below.

Why do you think the Torah is compared to a tree of life?

_____

_____

_____

Share your ideas with the class. What are some common responses or themes?

_____

_____

What Is Torah?

The word Torah (תּוֹרָה) literally means "teaching." The Torah is the first part of the Tanach, also known as the Hebrew Bible. TaNaCH (תַּנַ"ךְ) is an acronym for the three sections of the Bible:

1. תּוֹרָה *Torah* (Torah)
2. נְבִיאִים *Nevi'im* (Prophets)
3. כְּתוּבִים *Ketuvim* (Writings)

The Torah consists of the Five Books of Moses:

• בְּרֵאשִׁית *Bereisheet* (Genesis)
• שְׁמוֹת *Shemot* (Exodus)
• וַיִּקְרָא *Vayikra* (Leviticus)
• בְּמִדְבַּר *Bemidbar* (Numbers)
• דְּבָרִים *Devarim* (Deuteronomy)

The Torah is divided into fifty-four portions. Each portion is known in Hebrew as a *parashah* (plural *parshiyot*). In many congregations, all fifty-four *parshiyot* are read over the course of one year.

Each fall, following the holiday of Simḥat Torah, the annual cycle of Torah reading begins with the first *parashah* in the first book of the Torah, *Bereisheet* (Genesis). The weekly Torah portions then follow in sequence throughout the year, concluding with the final portion in the fifth and last book in the Torah, *Devarim* (Deuteronomy).

Many Jewish students study Torah from a *ḥumash*, the printed form of the Torah. The word *ḥumash* is derived from the Hebrew word meaning "five," and refers to the five books of the Torah. A *ḥumash* usually includes commentaries by rabbis and scholars that seek to expand or explain the Torah text.

Torah Mnemonic

As a family, think of a way to remember the names of the five books of the Torah in either English or Hebrew. For example, you could make up a short song using the names of the books, you could think of a sentence with words beginning with G, E, L, N, and D—the first letters of the English names of the books—or you could even make up a charade to help you associate the names.

Write your mnemonic here.

_____

_____

_____

_____

_____

Navigating the Torah

The following activity will help you become familiar with the way the text in a *ḥumash* is divided into books, chapters, and verses.

Using a *ḥumash*, look up the verses below and briefly describe their contents. In the space provided, write the name of the *parashah* in which each chapter and verse is found and give a one-phrase or one-sentence description of the contents of the verse.

For example, for Deuteronomy 6:4, turn to the book of Deuteronomy (the fifth book), and find chapter 6, verse 4.

Deuteronomy 6:4
Parashah: Va'etḥanan

Contents: The words that became the Shema prayer

1. **Exodus 20:2**

   Parashah: _____

   Contents: _____

2. **Genesis 12:1**

   Parashah: _____

   Contents: _____

3. **Exodus 15:11**

   Parashah: _____

   Contents: _____

4. **Leviticus 19:18**

   Parashah: _____

   Contents: _____

5. **Numbers 24:5**

   Parashah: _____

   Contents: _____

The Real World

When Mitchell Bild became a bar mitzvah, the Torah portion he read was *Miketz* in the book of Genesis. This *parashah* tells us of Joseph's imprisonment in Egypt. When Mitchell read *Miketz*, he thought about how lonely and helpless Joseph must have felt. Mitchell decided to focus his bar mitzvah project on helping someone he knew who was also feeling lonely and helpless.

Mitchell focused on helping Nicholas, a nine-year-old boy with autism. Mitchell saw that Nicholas suffered when he was ignored by other kids, so Mitchell made an effort to be a true friend to Nicholas. He invited Nicholas to his house and said hello to Nicholas when they passed each other in the park. Nicholas' mother has often told Mitchell how much he means to Nicholas, who now considers Mitchell a friend.

Discover Your Torah Portion

Explore your Torah portion together as a family using the following steps:

Step One: *Identify Your Parashah*

What is the name of your portion? _____

In which book is it found? _____

Step Two: *Examine the Text*

Find your portion in the *ḥumash*. Choose several verses that interest you and read them closely. What are the central ideas of the text you chose?

_____

_____

_____

_____

_____

As part of your bar or bat mitzvah ceremony, you will deliver a *d'var Torah* or *d'rashah,* in which you explain your Torah portion or haftarah and what it means to you. You may also talk about your mitzvah project (you will learn more about this in Workshop 4). Many teens also talk about the new responsibilities that come with a bar or bat mitzvah, such as reading from the Torah for the first time. Use the template below to guide you in creating an outline of your speech.

1. Summarize your Torah portion in three to five sentences.

_____

_____

_____

_____

_____

2. Explain how your Torah portion applies to your own life. Try to give at least one specific example.

_____

_____

_____

_____

3. In three to five sentences, describe how you feel about becoming a bar or bat mitzvah. What are you proud of? Worried about? Looking forward to?

_____

_____

_____

_____

_____

Parent's Perspective

As you prepare for your child's bar or bat mitzvah, think about your own connection to the Torah. Have you ever seen the inside of a Torah? Have you ever read from the Torah? Have you held or dressed the Torah? If you answered yes to any of these questions, how did it feel?

Focus on Text

הֲפָךְ בָּה וַהֲפָךְ בָּה דְּכֹלָּא בָה

Turn it over and over for it contains everything.

—Pirkei Avot 5:25

Each of the weekly Torah portions contains lessons relevant to our daily lives, such as pursuing justice and weighing our words before speaking. Perhaps at first glance your Torah portion was difficult to understand. Perhaps it seems to describe problems that are foreign to your family's modern life. However, as the Pirkei Avot text above teaches, the more we look at the Torah, the more we are able to connect it to our own lives.

As a family, look at the opening lines of the *parashah* that the bar or bat mitzvah will read during the ceremony. Now, read them a second time. What new lessons did your family discover after reading these verses a second time?

Reflections

As a family, discuss the following questions: Why is the Torah so important to the Jewish people? Why is it important to you? Jot down your thoughts below.

Finding the Sacred in the Bar and Bat Mitzvah Ceremony

Objectives

By the end of this workshop, your family will be able to:

▶ Explain why Jewish people pray

▶ Define an aliyah, including which blessings are said, when they are said, and who says them

▶ Differentiate between simply "wearing" and "wrapping yourself in" a tallit

▶ Describe how your family's celebration is a link in the chain of Jewish history

Lesson Launch

Think of a wonderful morning in your family's life. What made it wonderful? Perhaps you watched a beautiful sunrise after a night camping out, or you had a family wedding that day, or it was your own or a family member's birthday. Perhaps you were leaving on vacation. Describe the event and write one sentence about your family's feelings that morning.

Read the following lines from Yotzer Or, a prayer in the morning service—one that the bar or bat mitzvah sometimes leads. As you read these words, think about the morning you described above.

בָּרוּךְ אַתָּה יְיָ אֱלֹהֵינוּ מֶלֶךְ הָעוֹלָם, יוֹצֵר אוֹר וּבוֹרֵא חֹשֶׁךְ,
עֹשֶׂה שָׁלוֹם וּבוֹרֵא אֶת הַכֹּל.

*Baruch atah Adonai Eloheinu melech ha'olam, yotzer or uvorei ḥoshech,
oseh shalom uvorei et hakol.*

Praised are You, Adonai our God, Ruler of the world, who forms light and creates darkness, who makes peace and creates all things.

Why do you think that every morning in the Yotzer Or prayer worshippers formally acclaim God as the Creator of light?

_____

_____

In this chapter, you will take a close look at several blessings and prayers in the bar and bat mitzvah ceremony.

Why Do Jews Pray?

Prayer is a way of expressing ourselves to God. Tradition teaches that God gave us the Torah, and we responded with words of prayer in praise of God.

The Hebrew word for "pray" is derived from the root *peh-lamed-lamed* that usually refers to the concept of judging or judgment. "To pray," *l'hitpallel*, can be translated as "to judge oneself." This translation may be surprising, since we usually think of prayer as having to do with God rather than with ourselves. However, there are many types of Jewish prayer. Some prayers offer praise or thanksgiving to God, while others are personal petitions or confessions.

The translation of *l'hitpallel* as "to judge oneself" provides us with an important insight into a key purpose of Jewish prayer: prayers help us to look inward and to reflect on what is sacred to us.

Torah Blessings

Each *parashah* is divided into sections. For each section, one or more congregants are called up to the Torah to say two blessings—one before the reading of the section and one after the reading. The honor of being called up to recite these blessings is called an *aliyah* ("going up").

During the service, the bar or bat mitzvah publicly recites these Torah blessings for the first time and has his or her first *aliyah*.

As a family, read the English translation of the blessing said in most congregations before the reading of the Torah, then answer the questions that follow. Discuss your answers with the rest of your class.

> *Praise Adonai, who is worthy of praise.*
> *Praised is Adonai who is worthy of praise forever and ever.*
> *Praised are you Adonai our God, Ruler of the world,*
> *for choosing us from all nations,*
> *and giving us God's Torah.*
> *Praised are you Adonai, who gives us the Torah.*

1. The Torah blessing praises God "for choosing us from all nations and giving us God's Torah." What does this mean to you?

_____

_____

2. What obligations and responsibilities do you think the Jews have as a result of being given the Torah?

_____

Focus on Text

מֹשֶׁה קִבֵּל תּוֹרָה מִסִּינַי, וּמְסָרָהּ לִיהוֹשֻׁעַ, וִיהוֹשֻׁעַ לִזְקֵנִים...

Moses received the Torah from God at Mount Sinai and transmitted it to Joshua. Joshua transmitted it to the Elders...

Pirkei Avot 1:1

A first-time visitor to a synagogue prayer service quickly understands that the Torah is sacred. After all, it is housed in the Ark. It is dressed in ornamental garments. The congregation stands when the Ark is opened and when the Torah is lifted, and people often reach out with a tallit or prayer book to touch the Torah while it is carried around the sanctuary.

Tradition teaches that the Torah is sacred because it links us to the Jewish people and to God. When b'nai mitzvah read from the Torah, they recite the same words passed down from Sinai through generations.

In some congregations the Torah scroll is taken out of the Ark and passed from grandparents to parents and then to the bar or bat mitzvah. This act of passing the Torah from one family member to another symbolizes the passing of Jewish tradition from generation to generation.

Reflections

As a family, brainstorm ideas of how to make the experience more sacred. For example, you might examine other blessings or prayers that will be recited in synagogue that day. What meanings and understandings can you find in the words? If you could create your own blessing, what would it say? Use the space below to answer these questions and list other ideas.

A Lifetime of Mitzvot

Objectives

By the end of this workshop, your family will be able to:

▶ Explain the meaning of mitzvah and identify at least three mitzvot (plural) to incorporate into your family's daily life

▶ Describe the steps that will help ensure the success of a mitzvah project

Lesson Launch

Think about the commitments each of us makes throughout the year. We make commitments to our school, our work, our synagogue, our friends, our families, and ourselves. Maybe you're on a soccer team. Maybe you volunteer in a carpool or at a soup kitchen. No matter how old we are, we each make commitments that require our time, energy, and enthusiasm.

Join with two or three other families in the room, and share examples of commitments you have made to:

▶ Another person

▶ A job or class

▶ A hobby, cause, or organization

▶ Your family

In which area would you like to commit more time?

As b'nai mitzvah, we commit to living by Jewish values and undertaking the mitzvot. In this workshop, you will explore which Jewish values are most important to each member of your family. As a family, you will discuss how a bar and bat mitzvah project can help both b'nai mitzvah and their families demonstrate their commitment to Jewish values.

Hebrew Helper

Mitzvah is the Hebrew word for "commandment." It usually refers to a commandment written in the Torah or explained by the rabbis in the Talmud. You may already fulfill some of these mitzvot, such as lighting Shabbat candles, hearing the shofar blown, or sitting in a sukkah. These are examples of *mitzvot bein adam lamakom*—mitzvot between people and God.

There are other kinds of mitzvot, such as giving tzedakah, respecting our parents, and honoring the elderly. These are examples of *mitzvot bein adam l'ḥavero*—mitzvot between people.

These types of people-to-people mitzvot are also called "good deeds," but they are far more than just nice ways to behave: they are commandments in the Torah. Fulfilling them is a way of worshipping God. These mitzvot often involve behaving kindly toward others. For example, when you return a lost animal to its owner or give up your seat out of respect for an older person, you are both behaving kindly *and* observing commandments in the Torah.

What Matters to Me?

As a family, read the following list of mitzvot. Discuss and then place a check next to three mitzvot you each consider to be most important. Which mitzvot did you choose and why?

- ☐ *Bal Tash'ḥit* (Preserving the Earth)
- ☐ *Talmud Torah* (Jewish Learning)
- ☐ *K'lal Yisra'el* (Jewish Solidarity)
- ☐ *Tzi'onut* (Zionism)
- ☐ *R'difat Shalom* (Seeking Peace)
- ☐ *Bikkur Ḥolim* (Visiting the Sick)
- ☐ *Piku'aḥ Nefesh* (Saving a Life)
- ☐ *Zikaron* (Remembrance)
- ☐ *Hachnasat Orḥim* (Hospitality)
- ☐ *Kibbud Zekeinim* (Honoring the Elderly)
- ☐ *Sh'lom Bayit* (Promoting Peace in the Home and Family)
- ☐ *Ma'achil Re'eivim* (Feeding the Hungry)

All of these mitzvot reflect essential Jewish values. Now that you have identified which of these values are most important to you, think about what actions each of you might take to incorporate these mitzvot into your lives.

Your Heroes

You may know of people who are famous for their commitment to one or more of the Jewish values listed on the previous page. A hero from Jewish tradition, the second-century sage Rabbi Akiva helped others perform the mitzvah of Talmud Torah (Jewish learning) by teaching Torah to his students in spite of the Roman prohibitions against doing so. In modern times, Sandy Koufax acted heroically when he fulfilled the mitzvah of *K'lal Yisra'el* (solidarity with the Jewish people). As the star pitcher for the Dodgers, Koufax refused to play in the 1965 World Series game that fell on Yom Kippur.

As a family, think of at least two people you know who are dedicated to one of the values you ranked as most important. They can be members of your own family or your community, or public figures.

In the space below, write a few sentences explaining how these two people live by the value you have chosen. Then share your answers with other families.

Person: _____ Value: _____

Explanation: _____

_____

_____

Person: _____ Value: _____

Explanation: _____

_____

_____

Becoming a Hero

You can exemplify the values that are important to you. You have already taken the first step by identifying those values. As a family, discuss three specific things each of you can do to live by these values.

1. _____

2. _____

3. _____

Focus on Text

Why do people do mitzvot that involve acts of kindness toward others?

Today, we sometimes see such mitzvot as an insurance policy: If we do something nice for someone today then that person will return the favor tomorrow. However, the Torah advises us to understand mitzvot differently: We should perform acts of kindness whether or not they will have a benefit to us in the future. Why do you think the Torah describes acts of kindness in this way?

Chapter 19 of Leviticus outlines mitzvot that are both *commandments* and *instructions* on how to perform acts of kindness. Some of the mitzvot describe activities we should perform (positive mitzvot), and others describe activities we should avoid (negative mitzvot). Below is an excerpt from Leviticus 19. Put a ✓ next to the activities the Torah says we should perform and an ✗ next to the activities the Torah says we should not do.

The Eternal spoke to Moses, saying: Speak to the whole Israelite community and say to them:

☐ You shall be holy for I, the Eternal your God, am holy.

☐ You shall revere your mother and your father and keep my Sabbaths. I the Eternal am your God.

☐ When you reap the harvest of your land, you shall not reap all the way to the edges of your field, or gather the gleanings of your harvest.

☐ You shall not pick your vineyard bare, or gather the fallen fruit of your vineyard; you shall leave them for the poor and the stranger: I the Eternal am your God.

☐ You shall not steal.

☐ You shall not deal deceitfully or falsely with one another.

☐ You shall not swear falsely by My name, thereby desecrating the name of your God, I am the Eternal.

☐ You shall not defraud your neighbor.

☐ You shall not commit robbery.

☐ The wages of a laborer shall not remain with you until the morning.

☐ You shall not insult the deaf or place a stumbling block before the blind.

☐ You shall fear your God: I am the Eternal.

☐ You shall love your neighbor as yourself: I am the Eternal.

Why do you think the Torah includes the mitzvah of gleaning—the act of leaving leftover crops in the field to be gathered?

Why do you think the Torah lays down specific ways to do acts of kindness and doesn't just leave it up to the individual?

You probably noticed one phrase that repeats throughout the excerpt from Leviticus 19. It is neither a "do" nor a "don't" but simply a declaration: "I am the Eternal."

Our tradition teaches that this declaration is the reason we perform mitzvot: The Torah tells us that the mitzvot come from God.

Why do you think the phrase "I am the Eternal" is repeated in this passage?

Mitzvah Project

Many teens prepare for their b'nai mitzvah by doing a mitzvah project. The mitzvah project challenges b'nai mitzvah students and their families to ask themselves how they can perform more mitzvot in their daily lives.

Some of the mitzvot described in Leviticus 19 are not easily accessible to us today. Few, if any of us, have "corners of a field" where we can leave part of a harvest. However, we can adapt these biblical instructions to modern society. For example, we can collect the foods in the corners of our pantry to donate to a soup kitchen. If everyone took a few cans from the corner, the soup kitchen's shelves would soon be stocked!

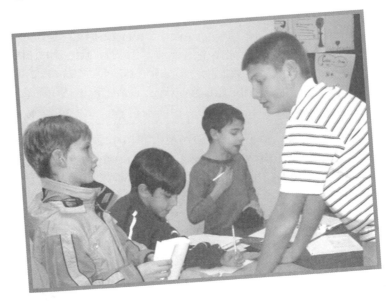

A-E-I-O-U

If you organize a mitzvah project in preparation for your bar or bat mitzvah, your synagogue may give you specific guidelines, or you may be free to choose one that moves you to action. Either way, strive to create a project that interests you and allows you to make a real impact.

When planning a project, remember A-E-I-O-U! The greatest projects are Active, Engaging, Influential, Ongoing, and Unique.

Active Imagine these two scenarios for your mitzvah project. One: You put a basket in the synagogue lobby marked "clothing donations." Two: You call friends and family, announce that you are holding a clothing drive, and offer to pick up garments they'd like to contribute. In the second scenario, you are *actively* performing a mitzvah and have a hand in your mitzvah project's success.

Engaging This is *your* project—let it speak to your values, interests, and hobbies. If you love dogs, volunteer for a dog rescue program. If you love sports, get involved in an after-school sports program for children with special needs. Let this project engage you! That way you will be more willing to invest your time to make it a success.

Influential Your work should have an impact on the recipients and perhaps even influence others to follow your example. For example, involve your younger siblings or family friends in your mitzvah project. Demonstrate that mitzvot can be performed at any age and whether or not you are preparing for a bar or bat mitzvah.

Ongoing If you pick a project that you enjoy, you are more likely to continue your project even after your bar or bat mitzvah. For example, if you volunteered at a shelter, the shelter will still need volunteers when your celebration is over. When choosing a project, be sure to consider how you can contribute your time and energy after your bar or bat mitzvah.

Unique Don't be afraid to try something new. Perhaps you would like to organize a mitzvah project that no one in your synagogue has done before. With the right motivation and support, you can dream big— even globally. For instance, you might want to collect money to send to an organization that distributes mosquito nets to African people who are at risk of contracting malaria.

Nate Evans had a good friend who lost his father to a form of skin cancer called melanoma. Nate decided to make melanoma awareness and detection in men the focus of his bar mitzvah project.

In his research about melanoma, Nate learned that men are most often affected on their heads and necks. Nate said that he realized that, "barbers work mainly with men, and view customers' heads and necks from every angle. With training, I thought barbers could be helpful in the fight against melanoma." Nate arranged for a doctor to talk to the barbers at the Busy Bee Barber Shop in Glen Ellyn, Illinois, about melanomas and how to recognize them.

After the barbers' training session, one of them noticed a suspicious mark on a client's neck and suggested that the customer get the mark checked out by a doctor. The man took this advice. He did, in fact, have melanoma. Because of the early detection, the man was able to undergo surgery and treatment that led to a clean bill of health.

TeenTalk

Below is a list of possibilities for your mitzvah project. Check those that interest you, or add your own ideas.

Bal Tash'ḥit (Preserving the Earth)
- ☐ Volunteer at a local forest preserve
- ☐ Start a campaign to reduce the use of plastic bags—encourage people to use canvas totes instead
- ☐ Plant flowers or pull weeds at a school, your synagogue, or a senior center

Other: _____

Bikkur Ḥolim (Visiting the Sick) and *Kibbud Zekeinim* (Honoring the Elderly)
- ☐ Visit non-relatives at a convalescent center or nursing home
- ☐ Put on a magic show, read, or play music for children in a hospital
- ☐ Take meals to a sick or elderly person in your neighborhood

Other: _____

Hachnasat Orḥim (Hospitality) and *Ma'achil Re'eivim* (Feeding the Hungry)
- ☐ Volunteer at a local shelter
- ☐ Cook and prepare a Shabbat meal for non-relatives in your community
- ☐ Organize a food drive for a food pantry

Other: _____

Tza'ar Ba'alei Ḥayyim (Compassion to Animals)
- ☐ Volunteer at an animal shelter
- ☐ Raise money to pay for an animal's care for a year at a zoo
- ☐ Volunteer at an animal rights organization

Other: _____

Zikaron (Remembrance)
- ☐ Read a book about Jewish history
- ☐ Learn from a Holocaust survivor about his or her story
- ☐ Find out if you are named after a relative

Other: _____

Tzi'onut (Zionism)
- ☐ Collect supplies for a specific organization in Israel
- ☐ Help with preparations for your community's Israeli Independence Day celebration
- ☐ Visit Israel

Other: _____

As your child pursues a mitzvah project, consider doing the same. Perhaps you will find inspiration in the list of Jewish values on page 32. Or consider collaborating with your child on his or her project. What better way to communicate to your children the values that are important to you?

When planning your own mitzvah project, keep in mind the criteria discussed earlier in this chapter. Like your child, you will have a more rewarding experience if your mitzvah project is meaningful to you.

613 Mitzvot

For most of this workshop you have used the word "mitzvah" in its broader sense to mean "good deed." Mitzvah also has a literal meaning: "commandment."

You learned on page 34 about positive and negative mitzvot. A positive mitzvah is an act we are commanded to perform; for example, Honor your parents. A negative mitzvah is an act that we are commanded not to perform; for example, Do not steal. Jewish tradition teaches that there are 613 commandments in the Torah. Why 613? The Talmud holds that 613 is the sum total of all the positive and negative mitzvot. Tradition teaches that there are 248 positive mitzvot, corresponding to the number of bones and organs in the human body. We also learn that there are 365 negative mitzvot, corresponding to the days in a solar calendar year. 248 + 365 = 613!

How many *negative* mitzvot can you name? How many *positive* mitzvot?

Workshop 4

Hebrew Helper

Se'udat Mitzvah

Almost all great Jewish celebrations include wonderful and plentiful food. The festive meal served at a bar or bat mitzvah is called a *se'udat mitzvah,* which literally means "feast of the commandment." A *se'udat mitzvah* is also part of other Jewish life-cycle events, such as a *brit milah* or a wedding.

Some scholars suggest that the tradition of *se'udat mitzvah* began in the time of Abraham. Tradition holds that the first *se'udat mitzvah* organized in conjunction with a bar mitzvah occurred when Abraham held such a feast for his son Isaac. In Genesis 21:8 we read, "The child grew up...and Abraham held a great feast on that day." The midrash suggests that Isaac was thirteen years old on that day, thus making the feast the first bar mitzvah festive meal.

Hiddur Mitzvah

The ancient rabbis also emphasized the importance of *hiddur mitzvah,* a practice that literally means "beautifying or enhancing the commandment." For example, when we use polished silver Shabbat candlesticks or wrap ourselves in a finely embroidered tallit, we enhance the mitzvah of lighting Shabbat candles or donning a tallit.

The rabbis point to Moses as a leader who demonstrated the value of *hiddur mitzvah.* They teach that when Moses led the Israelites through the Sea of Reeds and reached safety, he and the Israelites sang to God: "This is my God and I will glorify God." The rabbis ask, "Is it possible for a human being to add glory to the Creator?" They conclude, "What this really means is: I shall glorify God in the way I perform mitzvot." Moses and the Israelites glorified God in the way that they praised God— through a beautiful song.

When we practice *hiddur mitzvah,* we beautify the way in which we fulfill a mitzvah.

As a family, discuss how you can bring the traditions of *se'udat mitzvah* and *hiddur mitzvah* into your bar or bat mitzvah celebration. Use the space below to record some of your ideas.

How Is This Party Different from All Other Parties?

Unlike a birthday party, graduation dinner, or holiday barbecue, a bar or bat mitzvah party is the celebration of a mitzvah. The following activities will help your family think about how your party can be a true celebration of the mitzvah.

What Are We Celebrating?

As a family, discuss the reasons you will be celebrating. For each of the following items, mark whether it is very important to your celebration, somewhat important, or not at all important. Then add your own ideas.

	Very	Somewhat	Not at All
The bar or bat mitzvah can lead the congregation in prayer and can read from the Torah	1	2	3
The bar or bat mitzvah is growing up	1	2	3
It's a fun event in your family's life	1	2	3
The extended family is gathering in honor of the bar or bat mitzvah	1	2	3
Other (write in anything else that you might be celebrating):			
_____	1	2	3
_____	1	2	3
_____	1	2	3

As you plan the party, think about how your family can make it a reflection of the values you want to celebrate. For example, if, as parents, you have enjoyed watching your family's Jewish identity grow and change, perhaps you would like to mention this during a speech. Or perhaps you will offer a blessing to your child. If you, the bar or bat mitzvah, value your newfound ability to lead prayers, perhaps you would like to photocopy an explanation of a prayer that is particularly meaningful to you and distribute it to the guests.

What Makes a Party Meaningful?

Brightly colored flowers or balloons, lively music, and an assortment of delicious foods are all ways to add joy and delight to a celebration. Parties that celebrate occasions such as birthdays or anniversaries often have clever themes that reflect the honorees' favorite sport, movie, or hobby. Parties that celebrate religious life-cycle events, such as weddings and b'nai mitzvah, may find other ways to reflect the honorees' interests and commitments. Most especially, these are wonderful opportunities to share a commitment to Jewish life and values.

How will you make your party fun and festive while celebrating the mitzvah of bar or bat mitzvah? Some ideas include:

> ▶ Print the teen's Hebrew name, a quote from his or her Torah portion, or a Hebrew saying on the invitation.

> ▶ Connect the centerpieces to the mitzvah project. For example, for a toy drive mitzvah project, create baskets of games as centerpieces and donate them after the celebration.

> ▶ Plant trees in your guests' names to celebrate your family's connection to Israel and commitment to living environmentally conscious lives.

Use the space below to write your own ideas for creating a party that focuses on celebrating the mitzvah in bar or bat mitzvah. Be sure to revisit this exercise when you sit down to plan your party details. Share some of your ideas with the class.

The Guest List

Creating a guest list can sometimes cause stress and anxiety. You might be wondering, should all the teen's classmates be invited, or only close friends? Some Jewish schools have policies requiring the teens to invite their entire class so that no one feels left out. In other communities, the guest list is left to the individual.

Discuss which option is best for your family. Write your own views of this issue in the space below.

_____

_____

_____

_____

_____

Not only is it hard to negotiate which friends to invite, but it is also tough to decide which family members, colleagues, and community members to include. When making your guest list, you may wish to use criteria such as, "We will only invite friends to whose homes we have been invited and whom we have invited to our home," "We will only invite friends who know the bar or bat mitzvah child well," or "We're having a small party so we can only invite the closest family and friends." What criteria might you use for creating your guest list?

_____

_____

_____

_____

_____

How Will We Help Non-Jewish Guests Feel Included?

It is likely that there will be a mix of Jewish and non-Jewish guests at the bar or bat mitzvah service and celebration. Engaging non-Jewish family members and friends can be challenging. Ask your rabbi for help in finding ways to be inclusive. Consider that non-Jewish guests may find it uncomfortable or it may be inappropriate for them to participate in some aspects of Jewish worship, such as reciting the Torah blessings, which include the words *asher kideshanu* ("who has commanded us"). However, there are other ways for non-Jewish friends and relatives to become involved, such as leading a responsive reading or speaking about the significance of the teen's coming of age.

Below are three ways to help non-Jewish guests feel engaged:

1. Send out an information sheet describing the bar or bat mitzvah ceremony with the invitation.

2. Distribute a booklet during the religious service explaining the various prayers, ritual objects, and steps in the service. Be sure to have your rabbi or cantor review the contents in advance.

3. Create a Web page for the *simḥah* that includes comprehensive background information about the life-cycle event. Consider including travel directions and other event-related information on the Web site.

Discuss and then list three ways your family can help non-Jewish family members and friends feel included in the bar or bat mitzvah ceremony.

_____

_____

_____

_____

A Trip to Israel

Another wonderful way to celebrate the occasion of a teen becoming a bar or bat mitzvah is to take a trip to Israel. Trips to Israel, sponsored by Jewish youth movements, synagogues, and other Jewish community organizations, provide children, teens, and adults alike with an essential connection to their heritage, religion, and land.

The Real World

When Alyse Lichtenfeld went to Israel in honor of becoming a bat mitzvah, she had already been there twice before. This time, she dedicated a large portion of her trip to volunteering in different cities. Alyse brought with her a suitcase of new clothes to donate to charitable institutions. She spent time in several towns in the south, donating clothes and delivering presents to children. She also visited Kiryat Shemoneh, a town in northern Israel that has been attacked by Hezbollah, and spent time feeding and caring for the cats at the Reḥovot animal shelter.

Alyse celebrated the occasion of her bat mitzvah by donating her time to a variety of people (and animals!) in Israel. This trip, which Alyse took with her parents, allowed her to meet Israelis and participate in Israeli society. Even if you do not choose to volunteer in Israel, it is important to recognize that a trip to Israel is different from other trips. During a meaningful Israel trip, you will not only see tourist attractions, you will connect with Israeli culture, history, and people.

Has anyone in your family visited Israel before? If so, what was their experience? How might you plan a visit to Israel as part of your bar or bat mitzvah celebration? Write your ideas in the space below.

Focus on Text

רֵאשׁ וָעֹשֶׁר אַל־תִּתֶּן־לִי...

Give me neither poverty nor riches...

—Proverbs 30:8

Some people complain about the conspicuous consumption at b'nai mitzvah parties, while others delight in throwing elaborate, pull-out-all-the-stops affairs. The Book of Proverbs says that both extreme wealth and extreme poverty can lead one away from a righteous path. Both can distract us from the fulfillment of mitzvot. Do you agree? Why or why not?

Judaism does not encourage self-denial. At the same time, Jewish tradition rejects wastefulness and extravagance. Traditional sources tell us that it is desirable to be able to support ourselves and live a fulfilling and happy life according to our means.

Read the following statements about consumerism and check those with which you agree. Then, discuss how your community can support moderation in celebrating b'nai mitzvah.

- ☐ Consumer consumption is depleting the earth's natural resources.
- ☐ We should enjoy the riches we have.
- ☐ We should live for today and build for tomorrow.
- ☐ Wealthy communities are responsible for helping those who are less prosperous.
- ☐ All people should have the opportunity to prosper on their own.
- ☐ Wealth does not inevitably lead to happiness.
- ☐ Judaism does not embrace denial.
- ☐ Materialism may distance us from a spiritual life.

Gifts

When you become bar or bat mitzvah, your friends and family will want to acknowledge the event by giving you gifts. One of the responsibilities of becoming an adult is finding ways to give back to your community. As you are planning your celebration, you may want to consider asking your guests to make contributions in your honor to a charitable organization that you specify. Alternatively, you could ask your guests to bring items such as school supplies, nonperishable foods, or sporting equipment to your celebration for you to donate as part of your mitzvah project.

Reflections

Throughout this workshop, your family has discussed different ideas for creating a meaningful bar or bat mitzvah celebration. Synthesize these ideas below by listing five things you hope you will see at your bar or bat mitzvah celebration followed by five things you do not wish to see at your celebration.

I hope to see at my celebration:

1.

2.

3.

4.

5.

I do not wish to see:

1.

2.

3.

4.

5.

Living as a Jewish Adult

By the end of this workshop, your family will be able to:

▶ List three ways for teens and parents to stay involved with the Jewish community after the bar or bat mitzvah

▶ Describe three ways to live according to Jewish values

Lesson Launch

Imagine that it is the morning after the bar or bat mitzvah celebration. Slowly, each member of your family wakes up, and you gather for breakfast. Coffee is made. Bread is toasted. Orange juice is poured.

On the day after the celebration, how do you think you will feel? Describe your emotions on the lines below.

Teen:

_____

_____

Parent:

_____

_____

Although the event itself is over, becoming a bar or bat mitzvah is not the end of a process—it is the beginning of Jewish adulthood. In this chapter we will examine opportunities in Jewish family and community life that are available to young adults after their b'nai mitzvah.

If you are planning a mitzvah project for your bar or bat mitzvah, chances are it is taking a lot of time, thought, and energy. Remember that the need for mitzvah projects does not end the day after your celebration. One way to begin your life as a Jewish adult is to continue or expand your bar or bat mitzvah project.

List two reasons to continue working on your mitzvah project after your bar or bat mitzvah.

_____

_____

The Real World

Becca and Sam Israel, teenage twins from Northbrook, Illinois, exemplify how rewarding it can be to work for a cause that has personal meaning.

When Becca was five years old, she underwent surgery to remove a brain tumor. As a mitzvah project for her bat mitzvah, she collected art supplies for kids at Children's Memorial Hospital—the same hospital where she had had brain surgery. Becca has said that she considers it her duty to help other children in the hospital.

Becca's brother Sam also spent time at Children's Memorial Hospital when he was young. He decided to support an organization that saves the lives of many children and adults in Israel—Magen David Adom (MDA). MDA is Israel's first-aid and disaster relief organization. For his bar mitzvah project, Sam sent empty cans to friends and relatives and asked them to fill those cans with change. In all, Sam collected $478 in coins and put the money toward purchasing children's medical supplies like the ones that had saved him when he was a child. Sam further supported the organization by donating money he had received as bar mitzvah gifts.

Opportunities for Teens and Parents

After the bar and bat mitzvah celebration, there are many ways to continue to grow Jewishly together as a family. Below are three examples:

1. **Making a Minyan:** As Jewish adults, b'nai mitzvah and parents are all counted in a minyan. Become a family of minyan-aires—Jewish adults who help complete a minyan at a mourner's house or at a regular weekday worship service. Commit as a family to helping to make a minyan at least once a month. Feel free to bring along younger siblings so that minyan-airing is a family event.

    Why is it important to help make a minyan?

2. **Serving in Synagogue Together:** As a family, volunteer for synagogue activities, such as reading Torah, sponsoring or setting up a Kiddush, driving an elderly member to services, or helping to design and lay out the synagogue bulletin. For other ideas, ask your religious school director, rabbi, or synagogue administrator.

    In what ways can you contribute to your synagogue?

3. **Making New Traditions:** As a family, you can create your own Jewish traditions and rituals. For example, you could read a Torah story or watch a Jewish movie as a family once a month, bake ḥallah together for Shabbat, serve Israeli foods once a month, or add personal family stories to your Passover seder.

On the following lines, write at least two ideas for new Jewish traditions you would like to make part of your family life.

_____

_____

_____

Living Jewish Values

Living as a Jewish adult also means living your life according to *midot*—Jewish values, many of which are listed in Workshop 4. As Jews we are *banim* and *banot*—sons and daughters who have inherited the wisdom of centuries of sages and teachers. We are also *bonim* and *bonot*—builders who apply these values to our lives today and build for future generations.

As a family, read the following scenarios and discuss how you would handle each situation. Write your responses in the space provided. Then, join with another family and compare your responses. Discuss the ways in which your responses reflect Jewish values.

1. You see a dog wandering around a parking lot. It does not appear that the dog is wearing a collar or tags.

2. You notice a woman who appears to be homeless sleeping on a local park bench. You have seen her before but do not know anything about her.

3. After buying lunch at a local deli, you realize that you were given too much change.

I Believe

Adults and teenagers are sometimes confronted with moral dilemmas in which doing the right thing can be a challenge. When we are faced with difficult choices, we make decisions that reflect our values.

Your workshop leader will designate one side of the room "Yes" and the other side "No." For each of the following questions, think about the response and jot down a few notes. Then, go to the side of the room that most closely represents your view. Discuss ideas with your family and other groups.

1. Do you have the responsibility to jump into the water to try to save a drowning person when your own life may be at risk too?

_____

_____

_____

_____

2. Do you have the responsibility to give money to a homeless person on the street?

_____

_____

_____

_____

3. Do you have the responsibility to rescue an animal that is being abused or neglected?

_____

_____

_____

_____

Focus on Text

בֶּן חָמֵשׁ שָׁנִים לַמִּקְרָא, בֶּן עֶשֶׂר לַמִּשְׁנָה, בֶּן שְׁלֹשׁ
עֶשְׂרֵה לַמִּצְוֹת, בֶּן חֲמֵשׁ עֶשְׂרֵה לַתַּלְמוּד....

Five years is the age for the study of the holy writings of the Bible.
Ten, for the study of Mishnah. Thirteen, for the obligation to fulfill the
mitzvot. Fifteen, for the study of Talmud. Eighteen, for marriage. Twenty,
to pursue [a livelihood]. Thirty, for strength. Forty, for understanding.
Fifty, for counsel. Sixty, for wiseness. Seventy, for elderliness.
Eighty, for power. . . .

—Pirkei Avot 5:24

Do you think the stages of life in the Pirkei Avot text hold true in today's society? According to the text, can people live Jewishly their entire lives? Explain your answers below.

_____

_____

_____

_____

TeenTalk

What do you want people to say about you when you are twenty? Thirty? Eighty?

_____

_____

_____

_____

Reflections

We have reached the end of the final workshop. Now, spend a few minutes with your family discussing how the bar or bat mitzvah will affect your extended family and your Jewish community. What does this bar or bat mitzvah mean to the grandparents? What will it mean to future generations in your family? And, is there anything that makes this bar or bat mitzvah unique in your community? Jot down your thoughts below.

Conclusion

Mazal tov on completing the *Bar and Bat Mitzvah Manual!*

With this manual, you have taken the next steps toward a milestone in your family's life—the bar or bat mitzvah.

By investing your time in these practical and spiritual preparations, you help ensure that your family's bar or bat mitzvah celebration will not end when the last guest leaves. Rather, that moment will mark the entrance of a newly minted Jewish adult into a lifetime of Jewish practice, spiritual exploration, and communal responsibility. As you go forward, may you use the lessons of this handbook to create a bar or bat mitzvah experience that celebrates the best of your family, your community, and our tradition.

May your family continue to grow and learn together.